THE OFFICIAL
Heart of Midlothian
Football Club
ANNUAL 2009

A Grange Publication

Written by Paul Kiddie
Designed by Colin Heggie

© 2008. Published by Grange Communications Ltd., Edinburgh, under licence from Heart of Midlothian Football Club plc. Printed in the EU.

Photographs © SNS Group

ISBN 978-1-906211-34-9

£6.99

Contents 2009

CAPTAIN'S WELCOME

Welcome to the fourth full-colour official Heart of Midlothian FC annual – a must have for all Jambos!

The highlights of a roller-coaster season are captured in detail, including our famous victories over Hibs, Celtic and Rangers. The 2009 annual also looks back at our impressive CIS Cup run all the way to the semi-final at Hampden Park.

There's a special feature on the Thomson brothers, Jason and Danny, who describe what it's like to have sibling rivalry at Tynecastle – and having heard the banter between them it's interesting to say the least!

Lithuanian international Deividas Cesnauskis also gives a revealing insight into his life away from the football pitch.

Which stars of the past have made the biggest impression on you? John Robertson, Craig Levein, Craig Gordon or Stephane Adam? Many players have written their names into Gorgie folklore with their exploits in maroon and in this year's annual you can read about your favourite Hearts Heroes in a special feature.

As well as the legendary figures, what about the players coming through the youth system? You can read about the Ones to Watch in another in-depth section which turns the focus on players hoping to make the big breakthrough.

Hearts is a fantastic club and I am honoured to be a member of the team at Tynecastle. You can play your part as well - and together we can make things happen!

Roll of HONOUR

SCOTTISH CHAMPIONS: 1894-95; 1896-97; 1957-58; 1959-60

SCOTTISH LEAGUE RUNNERS-UP: 1893-94; 1898-99; 1903-04; 1905-06; 1914-15; 1937-38; 1953-54; 1956-57; 1958-59; 1964-65

SCOTTISH PREMIER DIVISION RUNNERS-UP: 1985-86; 1987-88; 1991-92

SCOTTISH PREMIER LEAGUE RUNNERS-UP: 2005-06

SCOTTISH FIRST DIVISION CHAMPIONS: 1979-80

SCOTTISH FA CUP WINNERS: 1890-91; 1895-96; 1900-01; 1905-06; 1955-56; 1997-98; 2005-06

SCOTTISH FA CUP FINALISTS: 1902-03; 1906-07; 1967-68; 1975-76; 1985-86; 1995-96

SCOTTISH LEAGUE CUP WINNERS: 1954-55; 1958-59; 1959-60; 1962-63

SCOTTISH LEAGUE CUP FINALISTS: 1961-62; 1996-97

VICTORY CUP FINALISTS: 1918-19

SCOTTISH LEAGUE EAST & NORTH DIVISION: RUNNERS-UP: 1939-40

SCOTTISH SOUTHERN LEAGUE CUP FINALISTS: 1940-41

TEXACO CUP FINALISTS: 1970-71

Club STATS

HEART OF MIDLOTHIAN FC THE HEART AND SOUL OF EDINBURGH

FORMED 1874

CHAMPIONS 1895, 1897, 1958, 1960

SCOTTISH CUP 1891, 1896, 1901, 1906, 1956, 1998, 2006

LEAGUE CUP 1954-55, 1958-59, 1959-1960, 1962-63

1ST DIVISION CHAMPIONS 1980

RECORD VICTORY 21-0 V. ANCHOR EFA CUP: 30.10.1880

MOST CAPS STEVEN PRESSLEY, 32 FOR SCOTLAND

MOST LEAGUE APPEARANCES GARY MACKAY – 515 (1980-97)

MOST LEAGUE GOALS JOHN ROBERTSON – 214 (1983-98)

MOST LEAGUE GOALS IN A SEASON BARNEY BATTLES – 44 (1930-31)

OFFICIAL WEBSITE WWW.HEARTSFC.CO.UK

OFFICIAL MOBILE SITE HEARTSFC.WAP.COM

OFFICIAL STORE WWW.HEARTSDIRECT.CO.UK

OFFICIAL ONLINE TV CHANNEL WWW.HEARTS.TV

Season HIGHS

MONDAY, SEPT 03
Motherwell 0 Hearts 2

Hearts registered their first win of the 2007-08 Clydesdale Bank Premier League season with an impressive 2-0 victory over Motherwell at Fir Park.

Laryea Kingston opened the scoring in the first half and Andrius Velicka clinched the points with his first goal of the season in the closing moments of the game.

Hearts 4 Rangers 2

The home side produced their best performance of the season to sweep aside the previously unbeaten league leaders.

First-half goals from Andrew Driver and Ibrahim Tall had Tynecastle rocking although a Daniel Cousin penalty early in the second half brought the visitors right back into it. Hearts hit back quickly, though, and a Michael Stewart spot-kick and an effort from Kestutis Ivaskevicius had the hosts in cruise control. Demarcus Beasley later netted a consolation effort for the Ibrox side.

Hearts 4 Falkirk 2

The Jambos were back amongst the goals with the visit of the Bairns. Audrius Ksanavicius set the ball rolling with the opener, compatriot Marius Zaliukas doubling the advantage before the interval.

Andrius Velicka and Christian Nade added their names to the scoresheet to set the home side on easy street. Two very late goals from the visitors failed to take the shine off a cracking display.

Hibernian 1 Hearts 1

The men from Leith seized the initiative with a goal in the first half, although that advantage was wiped out by Christian Nade's close-range finish moments after the restart.

Both sides created opportunities in a pulsating second half but with neither team taking advantage both sets of fans had to settle for a point at Easter Road.

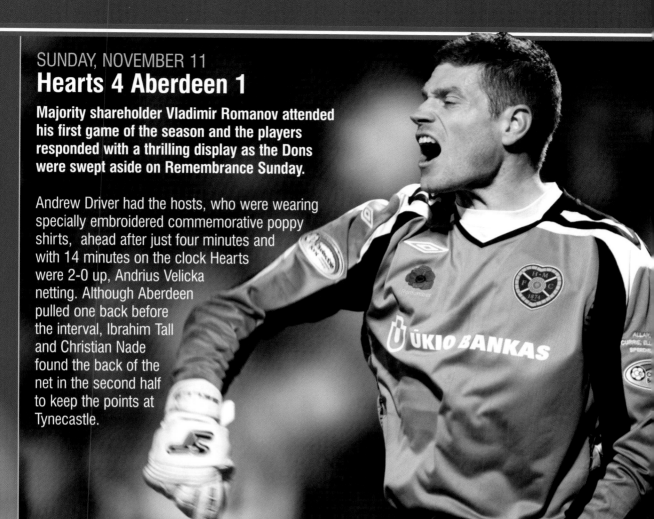

SUNDAY, NOVEMBER 11
Hearts 4 Aberdeen 1

Majority shareholder Vladimir Romanov attended his first game of the season and the players responded with a thrilling display as the Dons were swept aside on Remembrance Sunday.

Andrew Driver had the hosts, who were wearing specially embroidered commemorative poppy shirts, ahead after just four minutes and with 14 minutes on the clock Hearts were 2-0 up, Andrius Velicka netting. Although Aberdeen pulled one back before the interval, Ibrahim Tall and Christian Nade found the back of the net in the second half to keep the points at Tynecastle.

SATURDAY, DECEMBER 1
Hearts 1 Celtic 1

The Jambos staged a late, late show to earn a deserved point against the Parkhead side.

Things had looked bleak for Hearts after Anthony Basso's error had gifted the visitors the lead with just 18 minutes remaining, the Frenchman letting Scott McDonald's shot slip past him. Just when it seemed the hosts were set to head home empty-handed, Hearts were awarded a penalty after Gary Caldwell's foul on Ibrahim Tall. Andrius Velicka showed nerves of steel to slam home the equaliser.

13

SATURDAY, JANUARY 19
Hearts 1 Hibernian 0

With Stephen Frail having recently been appointed caretaker manager, Hearts basked in the glory of this derby triumph at Tynecastle.

It was a scrappy 90 minutes for the fans but the Gorgie faithful weren't complaining as a header from Andrius Velicka brought a 10-game winless streak to an end.

SATURDAY, JANUARY 26
Aberdeen 0 Hearts 1

Striker Christian Nade was the right man in the right place to score the only goal of the game as Hearts secured victory at Pittodrie.

Stuart Duff made a mess of a back pass to Jamie Langfield and the Jambos front man kept his cool as he charged down on goal and converted past the keeper with 55 minutes on the clock.

SATURDAY, FEBRUARY 23
Motherwell 0 Hearts 1

Eggert Jonsson played a significant part in this important victory.

The Icelander's first-half shot took a heavy deflection off Stephen Craigan as Hearts gained revenge for their Scottish Cup replay defeat at the hands of the Steelmen.

SATURDAY, MARCH 1
Inverness CT 0 Hearts 3

Hearts turned on the style as they strolled to victory in the Highlands.

Greek stopper Christos Karipidis opened the scoring with a header from an Andrew Driver corner and the visitors were 2-0 10 minutes later when Christian Nade's superb build-up play set up Calum Elliot who finished well.

The young striker, who had been low on confidence, then produced a magnificent finish to lift the ball over the stranded Michael Fraser and complete an impressive victory.

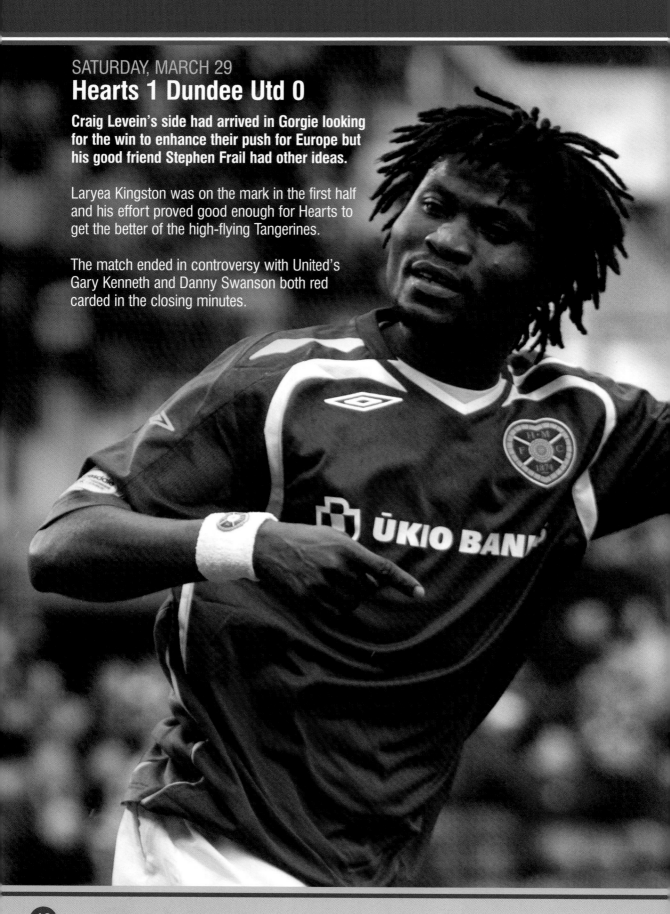

SATURDAY, MARCH 29
Hearts 1 Dundee Utd 0

Craig Levein's side had arrived in Gorgie looking for the win to enhance their push for Europe but his good friend Stephen Frail had other ideas.

Laryea Kingston was on the mark in the first half and his effort proved good enough for Hearts to get the better of the high-flying Tangerines.

The match ended in controversy with United's Gary Kenneth and Danny Swanson both red carded in the closing minutes.

The Road to Hampden
CIS CUP REVIEW

TUESDAY, AUGUST 28, 2007
CIS CUP SECOND ROUND

Stirling Albion 0   Hearts 2
Ellis og, Kingston

Given Hearts' poor start to season 07-08, there were many observers casting an eye towards Forthbank Stadium in anticipation of a cup shock.

With the Gorgie side having yet to register a win since kicking off the campaign with a 1-0 defeat to Hibs at Tynecastle, Hearts went into the second-round tie on the back of a 5-0 Parkhead hammering from Celtic.

Another defeat was simply unthinkable and there were to be no slip-ups on the proverbial banana skin, Hearts ensuring their safe passage with a 2-0 victory.

The all-important opener arrived six minutes before the interval. Good work from Saulius Mikoliunas set up Andrew Driver whose shot was well saved by Myles Hogarth. The ball rolled along the line and Albion's Laurie Ellis, in his haste to clear, only succeeded in slotting it into the back of his own net off the post.

The visitors doubled their advantage after the interval. Michael Stewart played a delightful one-two with Calum Elliot before the striker laid the ball into the path of the in-rushing Laryea Kingston and the Ghana international converted with a cracking shot which nestled in the bottom right-hand corner of Hogarth's net.

The second strike settled the nerves and although the home side had an opportunity to haul themselves back into the game, Steve Banks was on hand with an excellent save in the closing stages to deny Bell and prevent an anxious finale.

HEARTS Banks, Neilson, Tall, Berra, Goncalves, Stewart, Zaliukas (Karipidis 77), Kingston, Mikoliunas (Ksanavicius 64), Elliot (Velicka 81), Driver. **SUBS NOT USED** Kurskis, Palazuelos.

LARRY KINGSTON CELEBRATES HIS GOAL AGAINST STIRLING ALBION

TUESDAY, SEPTEMBER 25
CIS CUP THIRD ROUND

Hearts 4   Dunfermline 1
Nade pen, Berra,
Elliot 2

After extra time

The Pars proved plucky opponents for Hearts in the third round, the Jambos only securing a quarter-final berth with the aid of extra time at Tynecastle.

Recent signing Christian Nade put Hearts on the road to what the fans hoped would be a comfortable victory with his first goal for the club since arriving from Sheffield United. Calum Elliot was fouled in the area and the powerful striker stepped up to confidently convert the spot-kick.

Chance after chance followed for the home side but after failing to make the most of their opportunities in front of goal, the Jambos were made to pay for their slackness.

Former Tynecastle midfielder Stephen Simmons was the man responsible, his header six minutes from time taking the tie into extra time.

Home nerves were calmed, however, inside the first 15 minutes of the extra phase, Christophe Berra scoring once and Elliot netting a well taken double to put the home side on easy street.

HEARTS Banks, Neilson, Kancelskis, Berra, Goncalves, Kingston, Stewart (Palazuelos 29), Jonsson, Ivaskevicius (Ksanavicius 64), Elliot, Nade (Velicka 76).
BOOKED Jonsson.
SUBS NOT USED Kurskis, Zaliukas.

WEDNESDAY, OCTOBER 31
CIS CUP QUARTER-FINAL

Celtic 0   Hearts 2
Velicka, 2

Super sub, super result! Andrius Velicka stepped off the bench at Parkhead to clinch a famous victory for Hearts and propel the Tynecastle outfit into the semi-finals.

The best chance of the first 45 minutes fell to Celtic as half-time approached but Anthony Basso was equal to Scott Brown's thunderous shot, superbly tipping the ball over the bar.

As the second period wore on Hearts edged more and more into the match and found most creativity and success through Andrew Driver. The Englishman set up Calum Elliot who hit a great effort on the turn but Artur Boruc was well placed to save.

Hearts sensed that the game was turning and it was Driver who proved the undoing of Celtic's defence. On 75 minutes a Palazuelos pass found the Englishman in space on the wing and as he raced with the ball down the line the entire Celtic main stand screamed that it had gone out of play but there no whistle. Driver played on to the byline, cut the ball back for Velicka, who picked his spot and fired into Boruc's bottom corner.

There was even better to follow. Audrius Ksanavicius made a piercing run down the wing and found Velicka just outside the box and the Lithuanian unleashed an unstoppable shot which whistled past Boruc to seal a sensational triumph.

HEARTS Basso, Neilson, Tall, Berra, Goncalves, Driver, Palazuelos, Zaliukas (Jonsson 62), Stewart, Ksnavicius (Mikoliunas 88), Elliot (Velicka 71).
SUBS NOT USED Kurskis, Wallace.

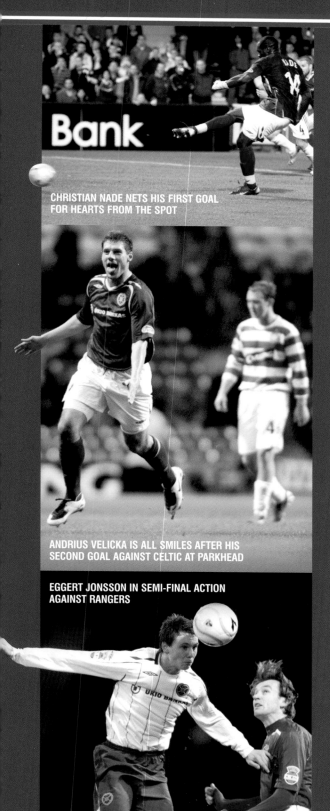

CHRISTIAN NADE NETS HIS FIRST GOAL FOR HEARTS FROM THE SPOT

ANDRIUS VELICKA IS ALL SMILES AFTER HIS SECOND GOAL AGAINST CELTIC AT PARKHEAD

EGGERT JONSSON IN SEMI-FINAL ACTION AGAINST RANGERS

WEDNESDAY, JANUARY 30
CIS CUP SEMI-FINAL

Hearts 0   Rangers 2

Completing an Old Firm cup double proved beyond Hearts with Rangers winning the Hampden showdown with two second-half goals.

Caretaker manager Stephen Frail was able to name an unchanged Hearts side for the first time since May 2006 but the Jambos struggled to recapture the form which swept Celtic aside in the previous round.

Controversy surrounded the opening goal, with Rangers skipper Barry Ferguson clearly controlling the ball with his hand before hooking a left-foot shot past the helpless Steve Banks.

The best chance of the game for Hearts fell moments later to top scorer Andrius Velicka, following excellent build-up play from Michael Stewart and Christian Nade. The striker's ball into the centre found the Lithuanian in acres of space but uncharacteristically his effort flew yards wide of Allan McGregor's goal.

It was to prove a costly miss as Rangers doubled their advantage with 68 minutes on the clock. Chris Burke got in behind the Jambos defence and his cut back left Jean-Claude Darcheville with the simplest of tasks to tap the ball home from three yards.

And with it went Hearts' dreams of a return visit to Hampden Park for the Final.

HEARTS Banks, Neilson, Karipidis, Berra, Goncalves (Wallace 84), Mikoliunas (Driver 59), Stewart, Jonsson, Palazuelos, Velicka, Nade (Beniusis 72). **SUBS NOT USED** Basso, McCann.

Brothers
IN ARMS

Footballing brothers Jason and Danny Thomson have a goal – to play in the same Hearts team.

Twenty-one-year-old Jason has already savoured life in the top team and his younger brother is determined to follow in his footsteps with the pair having travelled the same path to Tynecastle having both signed from Loanhead Boys Club as promising kids.

"I'm 21 and have been here since I was 11 years old," said Jason. "We both had season tickets and my dad used to take us to all the games so it's great that both of us are here.

"I signed for Hearts as I have been a fan since I was a kid. My first memory of a game is a match against Newcastle United at Tynecastle in 1995, which I think was Jim Jefferies' first game in charge. Ever since that day, I've been going to games.

"There has always been a bit of rivalry between us, no matter what we are playing. Neither of us like losing, although I'd say Dan's a worse loser than me as he has a bit of a temper!

"I never used to watch the U19 matches that often but with him involved, it's been good fun going along to see them and I think he quite enjoys me being there.

"Hopefully he can make it into the first team in the coming years and it would a dream come true for our mum and dad if we were both playing in the same Hearts team, especially if it was in a victory over Hibs!"

So what's it like having an older brother at the same club?

"Now that Jason has moved out of the house, I don't see that much of him and we just try to catch up during the week at the football academy," said 17-year-old Danny.

"To be honest he was one of the reasons I came to Hearts. I might have made the same decision had he not been here but he certainly made the decision much easier.

"He has been a big influence on me so far and it would be great if I could follow in his footsteps and get into the first team.

"Like Jason said, I'm sure it would be a dream come true for the family if we both played in the same Hearts team at some stage."

Word SEARCH

```
F  B  D  P  P  K  Y  C  R  M
G  O  R  G  I  E  S  R  M  A
L  S  F  N  J  L  K  U  P  R
E  T  T  T  A  A  I  B  N  O
N  R  Z  O  U  D  M  H  R  O
N  A  G  K  A  O  F  B  N  N
U  E  Z  T  G  A  G  H  O  K
T  H  S  B  N  M  Y  U  G  S
C  C  D  S  D  R  R  Q  D  T
E  L  T  S  A  C  E  N  Y  T
```

DUGOUT	GOALS	HEARTS	MAROON	TUNNEL
FANS	GORGIE	JAMBOS	STADIUM	TYNECASTLE

ANSWERS p61

At home with CESNY

CAR
Mercedes E55 AMG. I brought it with me from Lithuania when I came to the club. It is left-hand drive but I haven't had any problems driving round the city.

HOUSE
I live in an apartment near Fountainbridge in Edinburgh, while I also have an apartment back home in Vilnius.

MUSIC
James Blunt is one of my favourite artistes, while I also enjoy listening to Russian music.

FOOD
I enjoy cooking in the house when I have the time. My favourite meals are Chinese and sushi, while I often go for tuna cooked medium with rocket salad as well.

SPORTS
Badminton and tennis are two of the sports I enjoy away from football. I'd say I'm better at badminton, though.

COMPUTER GAMES
I have a PlayStation 3 and I like to relax by playing football and racing car games on it.

HOLIDAYS
The Maldives is probably my favourite holiday destination. I was there a few years ago and really enjoyed the diving and jet skis.

GIRLFRIEND
I married Vaida in June back home in Lithuania. We had been engaged for two years after I proposed on top of Calton Hill during the fireworks at the end of the Festival.

FILMS
Comedies are the type of films I really enjoy watching and Eddie Murphy is one of my favourite actors.

BAD HABITS
Well, if I am being honest, I like to drive fast, especially when I am home in Lithuania!

Meet the MANAGER

When Csaba Laszlo checked into Tynecastle in July, his arrival as the new Hearts boss marked the culmination of an exhaustive search by the club to find a new manager.

Better known to Jambos as the man former head coach John Robertson kicked at the end of a UEFA Cup defeat by Ferencvaros at Murrayfield in 2004, Csaba's CV is impressive.

He was head coach of the youths at Borussia Monchengladbach for five years from 1999-2004 where he groomed a number of international stars from an early age. After becoming coach of Hungary in January 2004, he also agreed to become head coach of Ferencvaros and he enjoyed the dual role for two years, helping guide the Hungarians into the Champions League and UEFA Cup.

Uganda then came calling in 2006 and Csaba soon masterminded a remarkable turnaround in the national side's fortunes, the East Africans soaring 76 places in the FIFA world rankings.

Hearts, however, provided a fresh challenge for the 44-year-old who was raised by Hungarian parents in Transylvania before he defected from Romania on a tourist's visa in the mid-1980s.

And he is determined to re-establish the Edinburgh side on the European footballing map.

"This is my destiny," he said. "I am proud to be manager of Heart of Midlothian. As a team working together we can achieve many things and it's important to get Hearts back into international football.
"Together we can change everything. 'Together' is the most important word in my coaching thinking. It is my intention to push this club in the right and successful way."

Married with two children, Csaba is fluent in at least four languages – English, German, Hungarian and Romanian.

Can you find your way to Tynecastle Stadium ?

Start

THE TYNIE TIGERS ARE IN A MISCHIEVOUS MOOD THOUGH, SO WATCH OUT FOR THEM TRYING TO BLOCK YOUR PATH!

ANSWER p61

SCOTTISH CUP QUIZ

1 In what year did Hearts first win the Scottish Cup?

2 Freddie Glidden captained the team to glory in the 1956 final. Who were the opponents?

3 Who scored the winning goal when Hearts defeated Rangers in 1998?

4 What was the venue in '98?

5 And who was the referee that afternoon?

6 How many times have Hearts been Scottish Cup runners-up?

7 What is the biggest crowd to watch a Scottish Cup tie at Tynecastle?

8 Who did Hearts beat in the semi-final in 2006 – and what was the score?

9 Hearts beat King's Park in the 1937 Scottish Cup to record their biggest ever win in a national competition. What was the score?

10 Who did Hearts play for the first time ever in the third round in January 2007?

11 What Hearts player scored a hat-trick that day?

12 What was significant about the 1998 final for John Robertson?

13 How many Scottish Cup finals have Hearts contested?

14 Against which team did Gary Mackay score four goals at Tynecastle in a cup-tie in January 1985?

15 Which goalkeeper played for Hearts in the 1968 and 1976 Scottish Cup finals?

ANSWERS p61

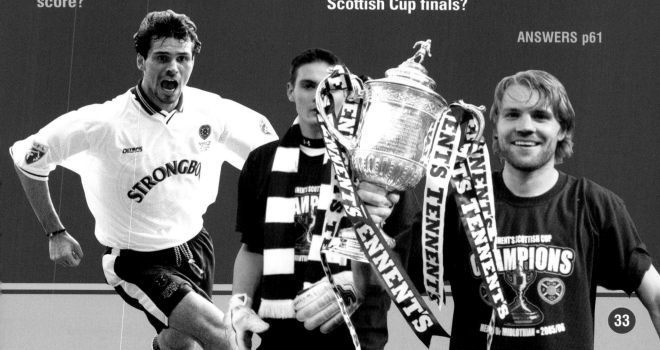

PROFILES

STEVE BANKS

POSITION GOALKEEPER
NATIONALITY ENGLISH
DATE OF BIRTH 9/2/1972
HEIGHT 5'11"
SIGNED AUGUST 2005
PREVIOUS CLUB GILLINGHAM FC
COMPETITIVE DEBUT 2/10/2005
OTHER CLUBS WEST HAM UNITED;
FISHER ATHLETIC (LOAN); GILLINGHAM;
BLACKPOOL; BOLTON WANDERERS;
ROCHDALE (LOAN); BRADFORD CITY
(LOAN); STOKE CITY and WIMBLEDON

ROBBIE NEILSON

POSITION DEFENDER
NATIONALITY SCOTTISH
DATE OF BIRTH 19/6/1980
HEIGHT 5' 8"
SIGNED OCTOBER 1996
PREVIOUS CLUB RANGERS BOYS CLUB
COMPETITIVE DEBUT 9/9/2000
OTHER CLUBS COWDENBEATH (LOAN)
and QUEEN OF THE SOUTH (LOAN)

LEE WALLACE

POSITION DEFENDER/MIDFIELDER
NATIONALITY SCOTTISH
DATE OF BIRTH 21/8/1987
HEIGHT 5' 11"
SIGNED JULY 2004
PREVIOUS CLUB
HEART OF MIDLOTHIAN ACADEMY
COMPETITIVE DEBUT 5/2/2005
OTHER CLUBS NONE

CHRISTOPHE BERRA

POSITION DEFENDER
NATIONALITY SCOTTISH
DATE OF BIRTH 31/1/1985
HEIGHT 6'3"
SIGNED APRIL 2002
PREVIOUS CLUB HEART OF MIDLOTHIAN
ACADEMY
COMPETITIVE DEBUT 30/11/2003
OTHER CLUBS NONE

MARIUS ZALIUKAS

POSITION DEFENDER/MIDFIELDER
NATIONALITY LITHUANIAN
DATE OF BIRTH 10/11/1983
HEIGHT 6'2"
SIGNED AUGUST 2006 (ON LOAN)
PREVIOUS CLUB KAUNAS FBK
COMPETITIVE DEBUT 26/8/2006
OTHER CLUBS FK INKARAS KAUNAS and FK SILUTE (LOAN)

CHRISTOS KARIPIDIS

POSITION DEFENDER
NATIONALITY GREEK
DATE OF BIRTH 2/12/1982
HEIGHT 6'1"
SIGNED JULY 2006
PREVIOUS CLUB PAOK THESSALONIKI
COMPETITIVE DEBUT 9/8/2006
OTHER CLUBS AO KAVALA (LOAN) and AO KERKYRA (LOAN)

JASON THOMSON

POSITION DEFENDER
NATIONALITY SCOTTISH
DATE OF BIRTH 26/7/1987
HEIGHT 5'11"
SIGNED JULY 2003
PREVIOUS CLUB
HEART OF MIDLOTHIAN ACADEMY
COMPETITIVE DEBUT 12/3/2005
OTHER CLUBS LIVINGSTON (LOAN)

BRUNO AGUIAR

POSITION: MIDFIELDER
NATIONALITY: PORTUGUESE
DATE OF BIRTH: 24/2/1981
HEIGHT: 5' 11"
SIGNED: JANUARY 2006
PREVIOUS CLUB: KAUNAS FBK
COMPETITIVE DEBUT: 11/2/2006
OTHER CLUBS: SL BENFICA; SC BEIRA-MAR (LOAN); GIL VICENTE FC (LOAN)
and FC DE ALVERCA (LOAN)

LARYEA KINGSTON

POSITION MIDFIELDER
NATIONALITY GHANAIAN
DATE OF BIRTH 7/11/1980
HEIGHT 5'9"
SIGNED JANUARY 2007
PREVIOUS CLUB FC TEREK GROZNY
COMPETITIVE DEBUT 3/2/2007
OTHER CLUBS ACCRA GREAT OLYMPICS FC; AC VENEZIA; AL-MAHALLA FC (TRIPOLI); HEARTS OF OAK SC; AL-ITTIHAD OF JEDDAH (LOAN); MACCABBI AHI NAZARETH; HAPOEL TEL AVIV FC; FC KRYLYA SOVETOV SAMARA; and FC LOKOMOTIV MOSCOW (LOAN)

ANDREW DRIVER

POSITION MIDFIELDER
NATIONALITY ENGLISH
DATE OF BIRTH 20/11/1987
HEIGHT 5'9"
SIGNED JULY 2003
PREVIOUS CLUB HEART OF MIDLOTHIAN ACADEMY
COMPETITIVE DEBUT 26/8/2006
OTHER CLUBS NONE

DAVID OBUA

POSITION MIDFIELDER
NATIONALITY UGANDAN
DATE OF BIRTH 10/4/1984
HEIGHT 6'1"
SIGNED JULY 2008
PREVIOUS CLUB KAIZER CHIEFS
OTHER CLUBS EXPRESS FC,
AS PORT-LOUIS 2000

SAULIUS MIKOLIUNAS

POSITION: MIDFIELDER
NATIONALITY: LITHUANIAN
DATE OF BIRTH: 2/5/1984
HEIGHT: 5''10"
SIGNED: JANUARY 2005 (ON LOAN)
PREVIOUS CLUB: KAUNAS FBK
COMPETITIVE DEBUT: 25/1/2005
OTHER CLUBS: SVIESA VILNIUS and
FK EKRANAS PANEVEZYS

DEIVIDAS CESNAUSKIS

POSITION MIDFIELDER
NATIONALITY LITHUANIAN
DATE OF BIRTH 30/6/1981
HEIGHT 5'11"
SIGNED JANUARY 2005 (ON LOAN)
PREVIOUS CLUB KAUNAS FBK
COMPETITIVE DEBUT 16/2/2005
OTHER CLUBS FK EKRANAS PANEVEZYS;
DYNAMO MOSCOW and FC LOKOMOTIV
MOSCOW

EGGERT JONSSON

POSITION MIDFIELDER
NATIONALITY ICELANDIC
DATE OF BIRTH 18/8/1988
HEIGHT 6'2"
SIGNED JULY 2005
PREVIOUS CLUB KF FJARDABYGGDAR
COMPETITIVE DEBUT 20/9/2006
OTHER CLUBS NONE

MICHAEL STEWART

POSITION MIDFIELDER
NATIONALITY SCOTTISH
DATE OF BIRTH 26/2/1981
HEIGHT: 5'10"
SIGNED JULY 2007
PREVIOUS CLUB HIBERNIAN FC
COMPETITIVE DEBUT 6/8/2007
OTHER CLUBS MANCHESTER UNITED,
NOTTINGHAM FOREST (LOAN), HIBS

KESTUTIS IVASKEVICIUS

POSITION MIDFIELDER
NATIONALITY LITHUANIAN
DATE OF BIRTH 17/4/1985
HEIGHT 5'11"
SIGNED AUGUST 2006 (ON LOAN)
PREVIOUS CLUB KAUNAS FBK
COMPETITIVE DEBUT 20/9/2006

RUBEN PALAZUELOS

POSITION MIDFIELDER
NATIONALITY SPANISH
DATE OF BIRTH 11/4/1983
HEIGHT 6'1"
SIGNED JULY 2007
PREVIOUS CLUB
RS GIMNASTICA DE TORRELAVEGA
COMPETITIVE DEBUT 12/8/2007

AUDRIUS KSANAVICIUS

POSITION MIDFIELDER/FORWARD
NATIONALITY LITHUANIAN
DATE OF BIRTH 28/1/1977
HEIGHT 5'9"
SIGNED JULY 2007 (ON LOAN)
PREVIOUS CLUB KAUNAS FBK
COMPETITIVE DEBUT 6/8/2007

CALUM ELLIOT

POSITION FORWARD
NATIONALITY SCOTTISH
DATE OF BIRTH 30/3/1987
HEIGHT 6'
SIGNED OCTOBER 2003
PREVIOUS CLUB
HEART OF MIDLOTHIAN ACADEMY
COMPETITIVE DEBUT 25/9/2004
OTHER CLUBS MOTHERWELL FC (LOAN)

MIKE TULLBERG

POSITION FORWARD
NATIONALITY ENGLISH
DATE OF BIRTH 25/12/1985
HEIGHT 6'1"
SIGNED AUGUST 11, 2008
PREVIOUS CLUB REGGINA
OTHER CLUBS AGF AARHUS, GRENAA IF

GARY GLEN

POSITION FORWARD
NATIONALITY SCOTTISH
DATE OF BIRTH 12/3/1990
HEIGHT 5'7"
SIGNED JULY 2006
PREVIOUS CLUB
HEART OF MIDLOTHIAN ACADEMY
DEBUT 17/3/2007
OTHER CLUBS NONE

CHRISTIAN NADE

POSITION FORWARD
NATIONALITY FRENCH
DATE OF BIRTH: 18/9/1984
HEIGHT 6'1"
SIGNED AUGUST 2007
PREVIOUS CLUB SHEFFIELD UNITED FC
COMPETITIVE DEBUT 3/9/2007
OTHER CLUBS ES TROYES AUBE
CHAMPAGNE; AND LE HAVRE AC (LOAN)

H is for Heart and soul of Edinburgh

E is for European adventures

A is for Adam, 1998 Scottish Cup hero

R is for Riccarton, home of Hearts' impressive football academy

T is for the Terrible Trio, Hearts' fabled strikeforce of Conn, Bauld and Wardhaugh

S is for supporters, the lifeblood of the club

Ones to WATCH

GARY GLEN

The striker exploded onto the scene towards the end of last season. He marked his first start for the club with his first goal for Hearts in the 3-2 victory over St Mirren in the Clydesdale Bank Premier League in April.

He followed that up with another goal in his second start, the youngster scoring the winner against Inverness Caley Thistle. Voted the Clydesdale Bank Player of the Month for April, the club has high expectations of the forward, who signed a new four-year deal in the summer.

RYAN McGOWAN

The versatile Australian featured against Barcelona in July 2007 but had to wait another 10 months for his competitive Hearts debut.

The Adelaide teenager, who can play centre of defence or central midfield, came off the bench against Gretna at Fir Park on the final day of last season and is determined to push on and establish himself as a first-team squad regular, having signed a new 5-year deal in the summer.

JONATHAN BROWN

The defender was knocking at the first team door for some time last season and is hoping to push on and prove himself capable of maintaining a place in the squad.

Signed by Hearts from Hutchieson Vale Boys Club at the age of 14, he can occupy either flank at full-back and has already represented Scotland at U17 and U19 levels. Another of the club's top prospects, who also signed a 5-year contract in July.

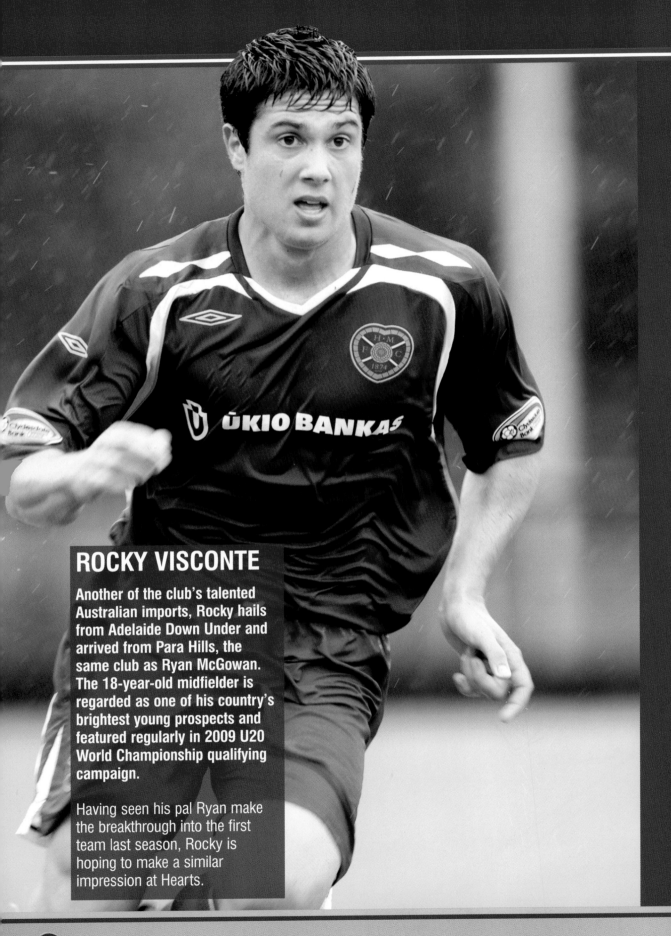

ROCKY VISCONTE

Another of the club's talented Australian imports, Rocky hails from Adelaide Down Under and arrived from Para Hills, the same club as Ryan McGowan. The 18-year-old midfielder is regarded as one of his country's brightest young prospects and featured regularly in 2009 U20 World Championship qualifying campaign.

Having seen his pal Ryan make the breakthrough into the first team last season, Rocky is hoping to make a similar impression at Hearts.

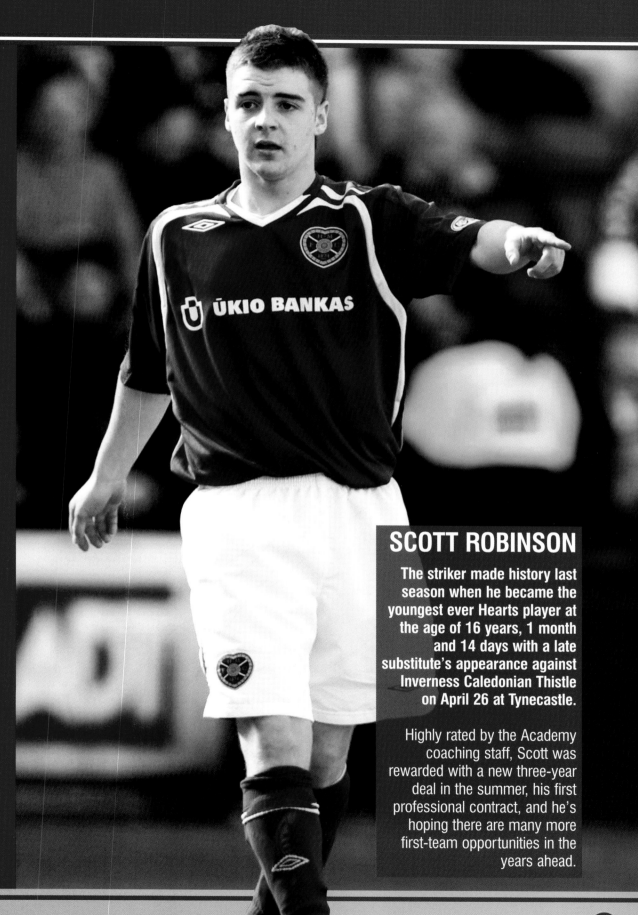

SCOTT ROBINSON

The striker made history last season when he became the youngest ever Hearts player at the age of 16 years, 1 month and 14 days with a late substitute's appearance against Inverness Caledonian Thistle on April 26 at Tynecastle.

Highly rated by the Academy coaching staff, Scott was rewarded with a new three-year deal in the summer, his first professional contract, and he's hoping there are many more first-team opportunities in the years ahead.

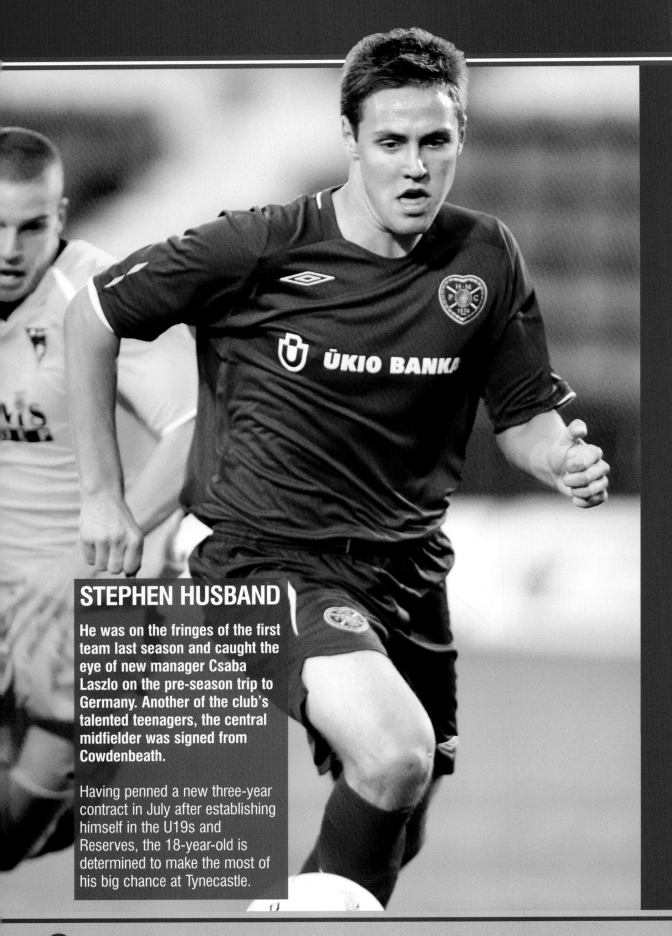

STEPHEN HUSBAND

He was on the fringes of the first team last season and caught the eye of new manager Csaba Laszlo on the pre-season trip to Germany. Another of the club's talented teenagers, the central midfielder was signed from Cowdenbeath.

Having penned a new three-year contract in July after establishing himself in the U19s and Reserves, the 18-year-old is determined to make the most of his big chance at Tynecastle.

CONRAD BALATONI

The 17-year-old has been with Hearts since signing from Fernieside Boys Club around five years ago and has made steady progress through the youth ranks.

The centre half was voted the club's U17 Player of the Year last season and will be looking to keep up the good work as he strives to make an impression at first team level.

It's all Greek to
CHRISTOS!

WHAT IS YOUR HOME TOWN?
Serres, which is in Macedonia in the north of Greece.

HOW LONG DID YOU LIVE THERE?
I was there for 14 years before I moved to Salonika

HOW OFTEN DO YOU GET HOME?
Footballers are used to not getting too much time off and I manage to get home once a year every summer which I always enjoy.

WHAT DO YOU MISS THE MOST ABOUT YOUR HOME TOWN?
My family including my parents and brother and sister are all there.

TELL US SOME OF THE PLACES A TOURIST SHOULD VISIT THERE?
To be honest it's not a very touristy place, although the weather in the summer is great and it's always nice to hang out at the streetside cafes and soak up the atmosphere.

ANY FAMOUS PEOPLE COME FROM YOUR HOME TOWN?
I wouldn't call him famous but Efstathios Tavlaridis is a defender who was on Arsenal's books before leaving in 2004. Angelos Charisteas, who plays for Nuremberg in Germany, scored the winning goal in the Euro 2004 final against Portugal. I lived close to Salonika and Theodoros Zagorakis who was the captain of the Greek team in Euro 2004, came from there.

WHAT IS THE MAIN FOOTBALL STADIUM LIKE THERE?
The team Panserraikos is quite a small team which is playing in the third division this season. Their ground Serres Stadium has a capacity of around 10,000.

AND THE BIG DERBY GAME?
There isn't really one as such and the Salonika derby between PAOK and Aris is the match which everyone is interested in.

WHAT OTHER SPORTS ARE POPULAR THERE?
Basketball is very popular. Football is still the No. 1 sport in Greece but basketball is next in line and a lot of people play it and it's a big spectator sport, too.

DESCRIBE SOMETHING YOU CAN BUY IN YOUR HOME TOWN WHICH YOU CAN'T GET IN EDINBURGH?
I really enjoy the meat back home and one of my favourite dishes is souvlaki.

Eggert Jonsson
MY BESTS

BEST GAME WATCHED
That has to be the incredible Champions League final between AC Milan and Liverpool when the Anfield side came from 3-0 down at half-time to win on penalties in Istanbul. Anyone who saw it will surely remember it for a long time.

BEST GAME PLAYED
The best games to win are the derby matches and the feeling when that happens cannot be described. The two victories over Hibs which I have played in are therefore the best matches I've been involved in.

BEST GOAL SCORED
I once scored from the centre circle when I was playing back in Iceland. My first goal for Hearts against St Mirren was a great moment, even though it did take a deflection.

BEST MANAGER
I don't mean to sit on the fence with this one but all the coaches I have had since I came to Hearts have been first class.

BEST HOLIDAY
Any time I get the chance to go home to Iceland and meet my family and friends.

BEST COUNTRY VISITED
Spain – it's a great place for chilling out on holiday.

BEST DRESS SENSE
That's a tough one – it's certainly not Christian Nade anyway – he dresses like a rap star!

BEST CD BOUGHT
Best of the Doors.

BEST WEBSITE
www.heartsfc.co.uk, of course!

BEST TV PROGRAMME
Friends

BEST FILM
Shawshank Redemption is one I have always liked.

BEST PURCHASE
My lap top computer. I can't go anywhere without it.

BEST CHILDHOOD MEMORY
All the summers when I was younger when I used to spend every day playing golf and football.

BEST SPORT (OTHER THAN FOOTBALL)
I really enjoy playing golf as I have been doing it since I was a young boy.

BEST THING ABOUT FINLAND
The landscape is really great and the blue lagoon, which is very popular with locals and tourists, is excellent.

BEST THING ABOUT SCOTLAND
Not the rain, that's for sure. The golf courses here are great and I really enjoy playing them when I get the chance.

Werner BURGER

Hearts assistant manager Werner Burger is a long-time friend of Csaba Laszlo.

The pair's friendship goes back to the time they spent studying for their coaching qualifications in Cologne.

Werner's former coaching positions include three clubs in Switzerland: FC Schaffhausen, Red Star Zurich (where he won the league in 1997-98) and FC Kreuzlingen.

Werner also worked with the DFB (German football federation) as a youth coach in the U15-U19 category.

Word SEARCH

```
X F L K D N D H R T H X
N B J F K N W R C Q N T
M R N E L O Q M Y M I D
G N O C F C T G H A E M
L N M B Q F L D J C V M
K R I M E I E D K K E V
G K T M D R L R M A L X
P G R D M U T H I Y J F
P R E M A U C S K E Z C
M N M B J P C Q O V S M
N R E K L A W T K N M R
M V M W A R D H A U G H
```

 CONN
BAULD

 WARDHAUGH
ROBERTSON

MACKAY
GLIDDEN

WALKER
CUMMING

LEVEIN
JEFFERIES

ANSWERS p61

Spot the DIFFERENCE

The Tynie Tigers were spotted outside the Heart of Midlothian Superstore. There are FIVE differences between the photographs – how many can you spot?

ANSWERS p61

Hearts HEROES

JOHN ROBERTSON

Born in Edinburgh on 2 October 1964, John is possibly the greatest scorer in Hearts' history, breaking a number of established records after he was signed from Edina Hibs Boys Club in January 1981. John made his debut in February 1982 and after he started scoring, he never stopped, eventually hitting 310 in 720 matches for the club. This might have been more but John went to Newcastle United in April 1988 for a fee of £625,000. However, he suffered injury problems and was delighted to return in December 1988 for £750,000. The Scottish International striker was the top scorer in the Premier Division in 1989-90 and three times he assisted Hearts to runners-up position. Hearts' ace striker also played in the Scottish Cup Finals in 1986 and 1996, and the League Cup Final in 1996-97. He had a brief spell on loan to Dundee before John finally earned a winner's medal when he was on the bench for Hearts' victory over Rangers in the 1998 Scottish Cup Final. John hit a club record of 214 League goals. In addition, he hit 27 goals against Hibs which is unsurpassed in the history of Edinburgh football. His management career has taken him to Livingston, Inverness Caley Thistle, Hearts (Nov 04 - May 05), Ross County and Derry City. He played 16 times for Scotland.

CRAIG GORDON

Scotland's No. 1 is currently ranked among the best in Europe and certainly, Craig's performances during season 2005-2006 were so often magnificent and were the key to Hearts securing a Champions League qualification place. That season he also made sure that the Scottish Cup came back to Edinburgh with a remarkable save during the penalty shoot-out against Gretna in the Final. Born in Edinburgh in December 1982, Craig came through the Hearts youth system and signed a full professional contract in 1999. He made his senior debut in October 2002 after gaining experience on loan to Cowdenbeath. A year later, Craig became Hearts' first choice after several match-winning performances, including a stunning display in the UEFA Cup in Bordeaux. In addition, in May 2004, Craig earned the first of his Scottish caps. Craig was Scotland's Young Player of the Year in 2002-03 and with considerable domestic, European and international experience he was eventually secured by Sunderland in August 2007 for a £9million fee. He was a popular choice as captain in November 2006 and had played 175 competitive games for the club before moving to the Stadium of Light.

STEPHANE ADAM

This popular Frenchman had outstanding mobility and skill, both on and off the ball, and the sharp striker also scored crucial goals during five years with Hearts. Stephane was born at Lille in May 1969 and developed his skills at the French Football Federation School, before joining OSC Lille. The 5'11" attacker then had eight years in Division Two with US Orleans, US Creteil and Amiens SCF, before a big move to FC de Metz in 1995. He earned a League Cup winner's medal in 1996 and gained experience in Europe before signing for Hearts in July 1997 under freedom of contract. Stephane made a huge contribution to the club's bid for domestic honours that season and although Hearts finished third in the league, his stunning goal in the Scottish Cup Final secured the famous 2-1 victory over Rangers. His goals also helped Hearts to finish third in 1999-2000, with his pace and passing skills being a feature of the team. Sadly, Stephane then had a long struggle to fully recover from a torn thigh muscle and he eventually went home to France in June 2002 after scoring 34 goals in 147 games (33 in 130 competitive matches). He subsequently gained a psychology degree and coaching certificates, and Stephane is now helping youngsters being a member of the academy staff at Lille.

CRAIG LEVEIN

Born in Aberdour in October 1964, Craig would have been the finest sweeper in Britain had he not suffered a series of knee injuries which required major surgery. The assured defender was a great prospect with Dalgety Bay Boys Club, Leven Royals and Inverkeithing Juveniles. He then played for Lochore Welfare Juniors before joining Cowdenbeath in 1981. Craig was outstanding in the lower divisions and was eventually secured by Alex MacDonald in November 1983 for an initial fee of £30,000. Craig was the SPFA Young Player of the Year in both 1984 and 1985 and a star man as Hearts came so close to the League and Cup double in 1985-86. However, he had to rebuild his career after two knee operations but did so in style and became an established Scottish international, earning 16 caps and playing at the 1990 World Cup Finals. With his strength, pace and skill on the ball, Craig became Hearts captain but sadly he was to suffer further knee injuries and was forced to give up playing in 1997 after 462 games for Hearts (401 competitive fixtures). Craig coached at Livingston before taking over as manager of Cowdenbeath in November 1997. He became Hearts manager in December 2000 and guided the club to third place in the Premier League in successive seasons. He left to join Leicester City in October 2004 but then departed the Foxes in January 2006 and after a spell at Raith, he was appointed manager of Dundee United in October 2006.

Tynie TIGERS

Fancy becoming a member of the Tynie Tigers club? Applying couldn't be easier. Just log onto www.heartsfc.co.uk and click on the Tynie Tigers link. Alternatively, call Elaine or Donna on 0871 6631874, option 5.

Being a member, you enjoy the following benefits:

- an exclusive Tynie Tiger membership pack.
- a birthday card.
- a Christmas card.
- opportunity to become a matchday mascot & lead the team out the tunnel at Tynecastle.
- quarterly newsletters with gossip and competitions.
- two signing sessions with the first team players.
- website competitions with fantastic prizes.
- news pages in the matchday programme.
- a voucher booklet.

SO DON'T DELAY, APPLY TODAY!

Quiz ANSWERS

SPOT THE BALL p19

MAZE p48

WORD SEARCH p28

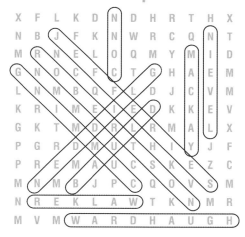

WORD SEARCH p52

SCOTTISH CUP QUIZ p35

1. 1891
2. CELTIC
3. STEPHANE ADAM
4. CELTIC PARK
5. WILLIE YOUNG
6. SIX
7. 53,396 FOR THIRD ROUND TIE AGAINST RANGERS IN FEBRUARY 1932
8. HIBS LOST 4-0
9. 15-0
10. STRANRAER
11. ANDRIUS VELICKA
12. IT WAS HIS LAST GAME FOR HEARTS, ALTHOUGH HE WAS AN UNUSED SUBSTITUTE
13. 13 – WON SEVEN, LOST SIX
14. CALEDONIAN FC (NOW INVERNESS CALEDONIAN THISTLE)
15. JIM CRUICKSHANK

SPOT THE DIFFERENCE p57

HEARTS U19s